The Friend Zone Destroyer: Escape The Friend Role, Have More Sexual Relationships And Become The Alpha Male All Women Want

By Dominic Mann

Table of Contents

An Introduction to the Friend Zone: The What, Why, and How

A Friend in the Friend Zone

A few years ago, a friend of mine (we'll call him Frank), got stuck in the friend zone. Not just stuck, but like *seriously* stuck. I am almost certain that the girl he was after (we'll call her Sally) was—at least acutely—aware of his intentions, but Frank just kept on digging himself deeper and deeper into the friend zone.

He showered her with attention. He texted her every day. He'd invite her out to the movies, tennis, and everything in between. He'd spend hours and hours calling her and skyping her, often long into the night. He got ridiculously long Snapchat streaks with her (and no, I can guarantee that Sally wasn't sending him any nudes).

In fact, he spent so much time being her "friend" that they even started to have some inside jokes.

Whenever he knew he was going to see Sally in person (often several times a week), he'd put on a nice watch, a nice cologne, and some nice clothes (above and beyond what he would otherwise wear).

He'd talk to her about her boyfriend troubles (and subtly try to give her hints about what a great guy he is compared to her "asshole" boyfriend). He'd be her emotional tampon when she was having some difficulties with her best (girl) friend. He, overall, was a great friend. But there was just one problem with that...

He didn't want to be her friend. He wanted more. He wanted to be her *boyfriend*. Her lover. But he was going about it all wrong. Literally, doing almost the exact opposite of what would have got him out of the friend zone.

I tried to tell him how to avoid the friend zone. I tried to show him the way out. But he ignored it all. He was stuck with preconceived ideas about what it is that truly wins a woman's heart. And it didn't work.

However, the fact that you've purchased this book shows that you not only realize what you're currently doing is not working, but that you're ready to change.

So buckle up and get ready to be catapulted out of the friend zone. You're about to learn how to go from having a "<u>girl friend</u>" to having a "<u>girlfriend</u>." (Yeah, that little space between "girl" and "friend" is also known as the friend zone).

<u>Why Do Guys Get Stuck in the Friend Zone?</u>

Most guys don't know why they're in the friend zone. "Why won't you luuurve me?" they silently ask.

Here's the answer: You're unknowingly doing things that keep you stuck in the friend zone.

Yeah, that's right. *You* are responsible for being stuck in the friend zone. It's not your friend's fault. Your friend isn't locking you into that dark, sad room known as "the friend zone" because they're a horrible person. You put yourself in there.

Don't be disheartened, though. There are two sides to this coin. Just as you put yourself in the friend zone, you can get yourself out of it.

So as much as guys love to make a fuss about how terrible it is being stuck in the friend zone, it ultimately comes down to this: You've either failed to make your intentions clear or she just doesn't want to sleep with you.

Put simply, if you get the Let's Just Be Friends speech, you can be sure that you screwed up.

Now let's get into the nitty-gritty.

There are two main reasons guys get stuck in the friend zone:

1. **The Friend:** The first reason guys get stuck in the friend zone is that they don't make their intentions clear. They just pretend to be a woman's friend and hope to dear god that she'll somehow be able to read their mind. If only I spend enough time with her, they think, she'll realize what a great guy I am. (This is what happened with the aforementioned Frank and Sally.)

2. **The Ugly:** The second reason guys get stuck in the friend zone is a little harsher: The girl just doesn't find you attractive. Women often try to be nice about it and so reject guys by saying, "Let's just be friends." (Please note that I'm not referring to physical unattractiveness. Women are attracted to specific behavioral traits, not so much physical traits like us men—which I discuss later. It's just easier to remember "the ugly" than "the behaviorally unattractive".)

"The Friend" is scared of rejection and so doesn't make his intentions clear. And no, by making your intentions clear, I don't mean spilling your guts and spewing emotional vomit in a big "confession" speech. I mean making your intentions clear through your actions—which is discussed later.

"The Ugly" has a whole host of unattractive behavioral traits (which he often doesn't realize because he thinks he's being such a "nice guy") that make women clench their legs together faster than you can say "oops". For "The Ugly" to escape the friend zone, he needs to start acting in a more attractive way (discussed later).

Often, the two go hand in hand. By the end of this book, you'll not only be able to make a smooth transition from friend to lover but you'll be equipped with the traits that make women go weak at the knees (and never dream of shoving you in the friend zone).

How Do You Get Out of the Friend Zone?

Guys get stuck in the friend zone because they fail to create a relationship. Sounds obvious, right? But wait, there's more to it.

You see, guys complain about getting the painfully familiar, "I'm sorry... I just don't think of you that way," or the, "I don't want to ruin our friendship."

But before you wallow in a pool of self-pity, pause for a moment. What do statements such as these imply?

Not sure? Well, here's what they imply: They imply that the guy is already friends with the chick. That leads only to one question: If you're sexually interested in a chick, why on earth did you become her friend?

Now, first, I want to make something clear: Of course I understand your plight. You didn't *deliberately* become her friend (or you at least didn't plan on remaining her friend). It just ended up that way. And you want to change that.

So... how?

Dive right in and discover for yourself.

Withdraw Attention

The Power of Absence

"Love is like a shadow, when you chase it, it runs away, when you turn back and walk away, it follows you."
– Unknown

Something that is constantly available is forgotten, taken for granted, and ignored by the brain. If you've ever worn clothes (which I'm assuming you have), you'll know this to be true. After having your clothes on for a while, you forget they exist. You no longer feel the texture of the cloth on your skin. For all intents and purposes, they might as well not exist (at least in your mind).

Well, guess what? You are exactly the same. Being available 24/7, answering text messages within less than a second, answering the phone on the first ring, and clearing your weekend schedule in case that special someone needs help moving—none of that makes her attracted to you. It doesn't make her want to sleep with you. All it does it end up with you getting taken for granted and forgotten.

If you *really* want to get her attention, disappear for a

week. Get busy. No calling her. No texting her. No being her emotional tampon. Just disappear into thin air (but that doesn't mean just sitting a home watching Netflix and eating ice cream, it means getting busy and getting a life—more on that later).

Now, there are two reasons that absence can prove so powerful.

First, it grabs attention like nothing else. In *The 48 Laws of Power*, Robert Greene writes the following for "Law #16: Use absence to increase respect and honor":

"Too much circulation makes the price go down: The more you are seen and heard from, the more common you appear. If you are already established in a group, temporary withdrawal from it will make you more talked about, even more admired. You must learn when to leave. Create value through scarcity."

In that same chapter, Greene also writes the following:

"What withdraws, what becomes scarce, suddenly seems to deserve our respect and honor. What stays too long, inundating us with its presence, makes us disdain it. Giving no reason for your absence excites even more: The other person assumes he or she is at fault."

We miss that which leaves while we take for granted that which is constantly with us. It's just human nature.

Here's a question for you: When does a celebrity make the most money?

Answer: The week after they die.

Here's another question for you: When does the household pet get the most attention?

Answer: When the family decides it needs to be put to sleep (i.e. euthanized).

Anyway, let's move on...

So what's the second reason that absence is so powerful?

The second reason for the power of absence is far less obvious. In fact, it's prehistoric. You see, us blokes have evolved to be attracted to a nice set of tits, a pair of long, luscious legs, a shapely butt, a symmetrical face, big eyes, clear skin, shiny hair, and all that good stuff. Why? Because all of these "attractive" traits are surefire signs of youth, health, and—most importantly—fertility. The cavemen that chased disabled old ladies, well... they didn't exactly get to pass on their genes.

Okay, that's all well and good, but what about women? After all, that's who you're after.

So what do women find attractive?

First, you need to realize that women grow the baby inside their bodies—not men—so women are, by definition, less concerned about a man's physical traits. So the question comes down to this: What increases a cavewoman's chances of successful reproduction?

Not sure? I'll tell you what. In a world of sabertooth tigers lurking outside your cave and buffalo's being hunted for dinner, the factor that maximizes a woman's chance at successfully reproducing is a man's behavioral traits. Can he catch the biggest buffalo? Does he have the strength to protect her (especially when she is pregnant and vulnerable) and her infant offspring from sabertooth tigers?

As such, women are attracted to a man's behavioral traits far more than his physical traits. What this also means is that women are attracted to strong, tough (both mentally and physically), dominant men. Or, put simply, *masculine* men—the alpha male. (As a side note, don't become one of those over-the-top dudes who's always trying to puff his chest out and out-alpha everybody else—that just reeks of insecurity and women can smell it from a mile away. But I digress.)

To put it bluntly, the wussy nice guy who was submissive and, well, just too damn nice, wouldn't have behaved in a way that maximized a woman's chance of successful reproduction. He likely didn't have the status or dominance within the tribe to ensure stability or secure resources. He wouldn't have been the best defense against the harsh conditions of evolutionary times.

So what does all this mean for you?

One of the reasons you're in the friend zone is because you act too damn much like a friend! Stop seeing her so much. Practice what Frank Kern calls a "pattern interrupt". Just get busy with life for a week and forget she exists. No calls, texts, or any of that business. Be a little unpredictable.

More importantly, this will increase your attractiveness in her eyes. No, I'm not joking. Being available 24/7 and clearing your schedule just to see her isn't sexy. You think the strong, dominant, masculine men (i.e. the type of men women are biologically hardwired to find attractive) would do that sort of shit for her? No! Of course not! Can you imagine Alexander the Great, Brad Pitt, James Bond, or whoever your male role model is, doing that? Nope. And neither should you (if you want her to think of you as more than a friend, that is). It all comes down to this:

Get a life, get busy, and stop obsessing over her. She'll find you all the sexier for it.

Stop Being So Damn Interested

Okay, so you've started getting busy with your own life and becoming less available. You're no longer acting as her therapist.

What now?

One of the mistakes many guys make is showing *wayyy*

too much interest. Not good. As we discussed earlier, women have evolved to want dominant, high-value men—not guys who obsess over her 24/7.

So show less interest. It'll help you get out of the friend zone and into her bed.

There are two ways in which wannabe-friendzone-escapees violate this basic tenet:

1. They become her official problem-handler. She have some problem going on in her life? Not to worry! Her "friend" will be over in five minutes to look after it. What a wonderful world (well, not for the "friend", but hey, that's his problem).

2. They refuse to keep their feelings to themselves. Due to their non-contagious illness, known scientifically as love sickness, they uncontrollably spew out emotional vomit about their "true feelings"—and it ain't pretty. All it gets you is an "Awww that's so sweet" followed by a kick into the friend zone.

Let's start with the first one. You know those guys who always want to make women's problems go away in the hope that women will see him as a hero or knight in shining armor? Here's the harsh truth: Women are in no way attracted to guys that act like that.

From a woman's perspective, he just looks like a needy, low-status, nice guy. Helping women make their problems better doesn't make them want to sleep with you. In fact, it does just the opposite—it keeps you in the friend zone.

Now let's take a look at the second way in which wannabe-friendzone-escapees end up digging themselves ever deeper into the friend zone: Spilling your guts with a big "confession."

Don't Spill Your Guts

In this book, we talk about having clear intent. After all, women aren't mind readers. So many guys get stuck in the friend zone because they're too afraid to make a move.

At the opposite end of the spectrum, however, are the guys who are suddenly inspired to make The Big Confession speech and reveal their "true feelings". While this certainly proves to be a big turning point for the guy looking to get the girl, it's not to his advantage. It takes him from potential boyfriend material to definite friend zone material.

And you know how women respond to this sort of emotional vomit? They say, "Awww that's so sweet" and kick him into the friend zone. Or, as the joke goes, when a girl replies with "Aww thanks", it means she's politely asking you to return to the friend zone that you just tried to escape from. Yeah, ouch. Not what you want.

So what should you do instead?

Simple. Keep your feelings to yourself and don't let your emotions get the better of you.

Nobody ever got out of the friend zone without keeping their feelings to themselves. Meanwhile, the guys who vomit out their feelings do nothing but dig themselves so deep into the friend zone that they eliminate any hope of turning the relationship into anything more than "just friends".

To start moving in the right direction, you have to stop telling her how "beautiful" she is. Just stop complimenting her, period. It doesn't make her think you're attractive. If anything, it just lowers your attractiveness in her eyes. After all, the type of men that women have evolved to get wet for don't act like that. They don't grovel at her feet and endlessly compliment her. So stop telling her what a perfect, wonderful person you think she is. Just stop. All you're doing is making yourself look lovesick and lonely.

Because most nice guys are almost certain to continue obsessing over and complementing their crush, I propose you follow the 50/50 rule. I would actually suggest you follow something more like the 80/20 rule, but the 50/50 rule is easier to remember and stick to. Here's how the 50/50 rule works:

- She says she likes you. So you reply, "I like you too."
- She says she misses you. So you reply, "I miss you

too."

It's really as simple as that. All you need to do is ensure you never take it further than she does. Otherwise, you just come across as needy and too emotionally invested—neither of which are sexy.

It's also important to only say something if you mean it. Don't simply parrot back what she says if you don't actually mean it. Also note that, as I said earlier, you can get even more out of this rule by taking it down a notch—such as by making it more of an 80/20 rule. In other words, show a bit less interest in her than she does in you.

Robert Greene is again a proponent of this in his book *The 48 Laws of Power*. He writes the following for "Law #4: Always say less than necessary":

"When you are trying to impress people with words, the more you say, the more common you appear, and the less in control. Even if you are saying something banal, it will seem original if you make it vague, open-ended, and sphinxlike. Powerful people impress and intimidate by saying less. The more you say, the more likely you are to say something foolish."

Greene also makes a point of quoting Ninon de Lenclos:

"Have you ever heard of a skillful general, who intends to surprise a citadel, announcing his plan to his enemy?

Conceal your purpose and hide your progress; do not disclose the extent of your designs until they cannot be opposed, until the combat is over. Win the victory before you declare the war. In a word, imitate those war-like people whose designs are not known except by the ravaged country through which they have passed."

Never reveal more than she does and don't spew out big emotional "confessions". Show your intent not through words, but action.

Be a Challenge

So far in this section on withdrawing attention, we've discussed why you need to stop being available so much (and why you should randomly disappear for a while every now and then) as well as why you need to "stop being so damn interested." If you thought all that was counterintuitive, you're about to be in for even more of a surprise. In this section, you'll learn why it is actually to your disadvantage to be "too easy" for her, and why if you want to escape the friend zone, you actually need to become more of a challenge.

First, let's unpack why exactly it is that women find guys who are "too easy" unattractive, while going weak at the knees for men who aren't so easy to get.

To understand this unusual (not to mention seemingly counterintuitive) phenomenon, we need to think back to our stone-banging, cave-sleeping, buffalo-catching ancestors. Do you think the strong, dominant, masculine men best able to ensure the survival (and thus successful reproduction) of a pregnant cavewoman and infant offspring would be an "easy catch"?

Do you think, to beat a dead horse, Brad Pitt, Alexander the Great, or James Bond (or whoever your male role model is) would be an "easy catch"?

It comes down to this: If you're "too easy", alarm bells start going off in a woman's subconscious. Suddenly, the subconscious says, "Wait, if he's so easy to get, is he *really* a powerful, masculine man? Could I do better? Doesn't he have other options? Are no other women attracted to him? He's just settling for the first woman he can get? RUN! This guy is *sooo* unattractive. Ew."

While most of these thought processes are subconscious and instinctual, they bubble up to the surface as, "I just don't think or you that way", "I don't want to ruin our friendship" and "let's just be friends."

When you're more of a challenge, however, the exact opposite happens—and that's what you want.

So let's take a look at some ways you can be more challenging:

1. Challenge her more. Most nice guys would never dare disagree with an attractive woman, and women know this. More than that, women find it highly unattractive.

After all, the dominant, masculine men they've evolved to find irresistible wouldn't give a crap about challenging a woman. This is also why women find so-called "bad boys" and "jerks" so damn attractive.

2. Don't be defensive. Defensiveness is an unmistakable sign of weakness and insecurity—two highly unattractive traits in the eyes of women. Women are hardwired with the instinctive urge to prod and test their men and reassure themselves that he is indeed the strong dominant man they should be mating with.

The second point is ultra important, so here is some more information on it.

Often these "prods and tests" come out as small insults (e.g. "You're just another one of those player guys aren't you", "*That* is your car?!", "How many women have you slept with?", etc.), although they can sometimes come out in even subtler ways (e.g. "Do I look fat in this dress?"—a question that both you and her know is stupid and pointless).

The way to pass these tests (more commonly known as shit tests) is to do the exact opposite of what your instinct is. That is, either just ignore it or nonchalantly agree and amplify what she says.

Here are some possible examples for all of the above example shit tests, in that order: "Sounds like you've got an eye for talent", "Yeah, hills can be a problem so get ready to jump out and push. You're strong enough for that, right?", "Today? Not many", "Looks like you just gained 400 pounds, take it off immediately. And your panties too. *wink*"

It all comes down to this: Don't be defensive, it just shows weakness and insecurity. Instead, show strength by having a nonchalant, zero-fucks-given attitude. Mess around and have fun with it, too.

Anyway, back to point number three:

3. Utilize the so-potent-it's-almost-magic power of preselection. Ever noticed that women, for some reason, seem to perk up and be more interested in guys that are already taken? You know, the guy that walks into the club with a hot babe on each arm, or the guy that already has a girlfriend, or heck, even a *wife!* Yet the guys that throw themselves at women seem to never have any luck. So what does this mean for you? Start dating some other chicks. All of a sudden, you'll find that your "friend" is *wayyy* more into you and that you just become all that more attractive in her eyes. (You'll learn more about preselection later on and how to use it as a jumping board to launch yourself out of the friend zone.)

You see, women want a challenge. It's in their DNA. If a guy is too easy, her evolutionary brain interprets that as him not being the powerful male women are instinctively attracted to.

As soon as their man stops being a challenge, a mystery,

exciting, and all that good stuff, women stop feeling that same level of attraction. And, more often than not, they move on. Or worse, the relationship turns sexless and the woman starts cheating on him.

The simple truth of the matter is that when you're too easy, her automatic response is to just chuck you in the friend zone. It's *not* to feel attraction. The friend zone can be thought of as a warehouse where she stores all the nice guys who've laid themselves at her feet and said, "I'm all yours!"

To avoid getting locked in that warehouse (or to escape), you need to become more of a challenge. Don't be "too easy."

<u>Kill Your Inner Yes Man</u>

Stop saying "yes" all the time. Seriously. Women, especially hot women, know that they can get their way with whoever they want. But the guy who can say "no" stands out and, at the same time, displays all of the masculine traits that trigger a woman's instinctive attraction.

Always succumbing to a woman's whims and giving her whatever she wants (or equally bad, trying to do what you *think* she would like) displays only weakness and insecurity. It just shows that you feel inadequate for her and that you're trying to compensate in other ways.

So what should you do?

Kill your inner yes man.

Later on in this book we'll discuss this in more depth by exploring why women love men who take charge and lead, while finding men who follow her orders and refuse to take charge—such as nice guys who say nothing but, "Whatever *YOU* want to do"—to be sexually repulsive.

So quit the neediness and kill your inner yes man.

<u>Say "No Thanks"</u>

This tip has more to do with avoiding the friend zone than escaping it, but it is important nonetheless. So what is it?

If a woman you're attracted to tries to put you in the friend zone or gives you the Let's Just Be Friends speech, just say, "No thanks." Simple as that. She'll either want to date you or you save yourself a ton of time masquerading as a friend.

Take Charge and Lead

Take the Masculine Role

Many a nice guy fall into an easy to miss trap: The trap of failing to take the masculine role in the relationship.

Just as batteries require a negative and positive pole to create energy, and magnets require likewise to attract each other, so too do relationships require both a masculine and feminine role for there to be intense attraction.

Unfortunately, many nice guys slip not into the masculine role but into the role of an androgynous drone. Instead of taking charge, they just ask, "What do *YOU* want to do?" There really is little that women hate more than being asked that question. Moreover, there's little more that kills attraction.

This is yet *another* reason that women find themselves unable to resist bad boys and jerks. These guys are unabashedly masculine and take charge of the relationship without hesitation.

The wussy nice guy's on the other hand? They refuse to

take charge, falsely thinking that they can make a woman happier by just tagging along as she does whatever she wants. But that's completely wrong. It's back to front. Women want *you* to lead.

This is why it is so important to live your own life. Women *do not*–let me repeat: do *not*–want to be the center of your life. They don't want to be put on a pedestal and worshiped. They want nothing of the sort. If anything, they want just the *opposite*.

They want a man who has an exciting lifestyle and who lives life as an adventure. They don't want a man who creepily obsesses over women and makes that "special someone" the center of his life. Yuck.

They want to tag along with a dominant man as he goes about living an exciting life. And yes, that word choice was specific. Women want to *tag along*. Not order her man around. Not have her man do whatever she wants to do. Not have her man follow her around like a lost dog. They want a man who's on a mission, who has a definite direction and an exciting purpose, and they want to tag along.

Going a little off topic, this is why women shit test you (as briefly discussed earlier). They want to feel that you are unshakeable. That's incredibly sexy for women. Not that you collapse to their will and act on her every whim. That's, well, to put it bluntly, sexually repulsive in a woman's mind.

But let's get back on topic. You see, handing over the reins and letting her make all the decisions, call the shots, and take the lead makes her view you as less of a man. Women are instinctively attracted to men who take charge without thinking twice about it.

Instead of taking the usual "What do *YOU* want to do?" nice guy mindset, take the mindset of "I'm doing XYZ. Feel free to tag along."

Still not convinced that women don't want to *be* your life? That they'd rather you have your own exciting life and just tag along on your adventures?

Then go walk into your local bookstore (or search the Amazon Kindle Store). You'll find no shortage of erotica (i.e. women's porn) about bikies, billionaires, and other such bad boys—just to name some of the B's. Take a flip through *50 Shades of Grey* and you'll realize that millions of women around the world have been fantasizing about a man taking charge and being extraordinarily dominant without thinking twice about it.

Nice guys, on the other hand... well, I'll tell you this now: You're not going to find any erotica about nice guys who make women the center of their life, force women to choose what they want to do, and do nothing exciting or have no life of their own.

Stop Being Submissive

Do you know how to make a girl automatically throw you in the friend zone?

Be submissive.

That's why if you want to find a herd of eager-to-please nice guys, all you need to do is go take a look in the friend zone.

Conversely, doing just the opposite will have equally opposite results. That is, be dominant. Be the alpha. Be confident and take charge.

Don't act like her servant. Don't kiss her feet. Don't worship her. Don't be submissive.

Destroy the Pedestal, Be the Leader

To drive this point home and help it stick in your mind, here are two examples from TV shows/movies you might have seen.

First, *House of Cards*. In the sixth episode of the first season, Claire Underwood—the wife of Machiavellian (i.e. cutthroat, ruthless, *asshole*) congressman Frank Underwood—visits Frank's former bodyguard in hospital. The bodyguard, named Steve, now has cancer, is stuck in hospital, and will soon die.

So Steve sends Claire a text message asking her to visit him and takes the opportunity to confess his love for her. Probably expecting sympathy, he got something else entirely. Here's the conversation:

Steve: *I hate your husband.*

Claire: *A lot of people do.*

Steve: *The past eight years I watched over him. But it wasn't him I was watching. And every time I saw you, every time I heard your voice, all I could think to myself was 'Jesus what I would give'... I can't tell you how many times I thought about that.*

Claire: *You know what Francis said to me when he proposed? I remember his exact words. He said, 'Claire, if all you want is happiness, say no. I'm not gonna give you a couple of kids and count the days until retirement. I promise you freedom from that. I promise you'll never be bored.'*

And you know, he was the only man, and there were a lot of others who proposed, he was the only one who understood me. He didn't put me on some pedestal. He knew that I didn't want to be adored or coddled. So he took my hand and he put a ring on it...because he knew I would say yes. He's a man who knows how to take what he wants.

What's the lesson? Women don't want to be put on a pedestal. They don't want a white knight. They don't want a servant. They don't want a submissive nice guy who obsesses over her and makes her the center of their life. They want a *man*.

Finally, *The Tourist*. I haven't seen the movie myself, but plenty of people have shown me a conversation from the film which does a great job of demonstrating the fact that women want a man who takes charge and leads. A man who lives his own exciting life and let's women be feminine and tag along rather than shrugging the masculine role onto them with the attraction-killing "What *you* want to do?" Here it is:

Elise: *Invite me to dinner, Frank?*

Frank Taylor: *What?*

Elise: *[gives him a look]*

Frank Taylor: *Would you like to have dinner?*

Elise: *Women don't like questions.*

Frank Taylor: *Join me for dinner.*

Elise: *Too demanding.*

Frank Taylor: *Join me for dinner?*

Elise: *Another question.*

Frank Taylor: *[thinks for a moment] I'm having dinner, if you'd care to join me.*

Elise: *[smiles at him]*

Although these examples originate not from reality but the pencil of a screenwriter, you will find that they hold very real truths that hopefully stick in your mind.

How to Flirt Your Way Out of the Friend Zone

<u>The Fundamentals of Flirting</u>

In this book we discuss the importance of making your intentions clear not through words (i.e. The Big Confession speech) but actions—many of which are discussed later on in the book. One of the essential parts to this is *flirting*. So let's take a look at the definition:

flirt
verb

1. behave as if sexually attracted to someone, but playfully rather than with serious intentions.
   "she began to tease him, flirting with other men in front of him"

The most important part of this definition are the words "playfully rather than with serious intentions." That is the essence of flirting. A push and then a pull. A "you're too cute to handle, shoo *shove*" or a "go away a little closer" kind of thing.

Push-Pull and Chase Framing

On top of this push-pull dynamic, you can playfully frame the conversation as if she's the one trying to seduce you. As if she's the one chasing you (this is known as "chase framing," coined by Chase Armante at http://girlschase.com/). For example, she might say, "There's nothing better than a good massage," to which you could reply, "Trying to seduce me with a massage?"

The biggest mistake guys make when it comes to flirting is being too obvious. That's not flirty, it's creepy. The secret is to be subtle. Imply things rather than state things directly. This can be a little difficult to get used to as us guys are so used to being direct when communicating, but it is nonetheless essential to good flirting.

Preselection

What is preselection?

Preselection is, put simply, when a man is "preselected" by other attractive women. In other words, other hot women find a man attractive. This is why if you go into any bar or club, you'll find that women are most interested in the guy that all the other women are interested in. Women find a man who has options very sexy. A man who doesn't have any options (i.e. is needy, desperate, an obvious and insecure virgin, friend zoned by every woman he knows, etc.) to be incredibly unattractive.

Why is this? After all, us guys seem to be the opposite. We're not hardwired to be attracted to women who get f*cked every other day or get passed around like a bong at a party. If anything, guys enjoy being the first to bed a virgin.

As you might have guessed, it once again all comes down to evolution.

For women, there's a lot at stake. Getting impregnated by a weak wussy nice guy in prehistoric times meant almost certain death. He wouldn't be able to protect and provide for her when she's pregnant and vulnerable, let alone ensure the survival of the infant offspring.

For us guys, though, it's not a big deal. If we accidentally knock up the wrong woman, no worries. Leave it 15 minutes and we can go try another woman.

Unfortunately for women, though, determining whether a guy is the strong, dominant, masculine guy she's after takes a lot of work. After all, a lot of guys who are, at heart, wussy weaklings, pretend to be big, tough, alpha males. (As a side note, this is another reason why women shit test men as discussed earlier.)

But what's a surefire way to determine whether a guy has all the traits she's looking for?

Preselection. If other women are all over a guy, there's a good chance he's the type of guy who can—in prehistoric terms —maximize her chances of successful reproduction. In modern day terms, a guy who's damn sexy. (Remember: Yes, I know I've said it before, but I want to make sure I get it into your head. What a woman finds "sexy" is a man with powerful, dominant behavior. While six-pack abs are nice, they're not going to help you with women if you don't have the fundamentals down.)

A guy who's willing and able to walk away demonstrates he has options. And women find that ridiculously attractive.

If you're still not convinced of the incredible leg-unlocking, friend zone disappearing powers of preselection (which is arguably the NUMBER ONE biggest thing you can do to dramatically increase your attractiveness in the eyes of women), then listen up. Study, after study, after study has found that women find guys that *other* women find attractive far, far, far more attractive. And no, it's not just because the guy is already attractive (and that's why other women are attracted to him). In these studies, they got showed *the very same guy.* Heck, one study found that simply pointing a *separate* (i.e. totally unrelated) picture of a smiling woman at a photo of an ordinary looking guy made him far more attractive in the eyes of women. Yeah, seriously. This stuff works.

But what does this mean for you? What does this have to do with escaping the friend zone?

Simple. Go date other chicks.

But wait, you say, won't that do just the opposite of what you want?

The counterintuitive answer is that no, it will actually make her *stop* seeing you as friend zone material, and instead, see you as something more—which is what you want. More than that, it will skyrocket your attractiveness in her eyes.

In fact, I would go so far as to argue that the *best* way to escape the friend zone is to let her see you dating and attracting other women. However, it is important to note that they must be attractive women. If you go around dating ugly women, it is going to have the exact opposite effect.

Go to a party or two. Approach some women. Get an attractive girl's phone number in front of her (i.e. your "friend"– don't pay her any attention, though, just pretend she doesn't exist). Date a few other women. Post pictures on Facebook of you and a few pretty girls. And so on.

When your "friend" starts mentioning these girls (which she will often do as a passive aggressive insult or tease), just playfully tease her about being jealous, etc. Yes, *playfully.* Don't get all defensive or aggressive. Just be very casual and nonchalant. Have a bit of fun. Show a little amusement.

While preselection is the single biggest female attraction trigger, there's one common mistake that a lot of guys make that kill (or at least significantly decrease) it's effectiveness.

What is it?

The Big Tell All. This mistake looks very similar to another friend zone mistake: The Big Confession speech (which we discussed earlier).

So what is The Big Tell All?

The Big Tell All happens when you finally get some preselection going, you've got some hot girls you're dating who are clearly attracted to you, and your "friend" starts getting antsy about it. She will (likely) start probing for details and start subtly insulting the girls you're with.

And so what happens?

The nice guy decides to tell her everything. Everything from meeting the other girls to the exact time and location of any dates to what they did together and whether the nice guy got any action.

But why is this bad, you ask?

Because it kills the mystery. She's no longer curious. She's no longer thinking about it and wondering what happened. The power that this kind of preselection would have otherwise had to catapult you right out of the friend zone just disappears. By telling her the details, you destroy that fantasy she has in her head.

So don't give her the details. Just keep it mysterious. If you do, she *will* imagine that you're having much more success with women than you actually are. Which, in turn, will make you ridiculously sexy in her mind. So say no more than "Yeah, I'm seeing other women. Anyway, tell me about [change topic]." No reality can match the fantasy she builds in her head.

If she mentions it and you say, "Yeah, I'm seeing other women," for all she knows, you're seeing seven different smoking hot babes and banging them all every other day— which means your preselection (and thus your sexual attractiveness) will go through the roof. If you give her the details and say, "Yeah, I went on one date with a girl named Emily, which was nice," then you've just sucked all the mystery out of it. Nothing is left to the imagination. There's no mystery, jealousy, or competition.

The vaguer and more mysterious, the better. Remember: Give her too many details and you'll end up like the sexless husband—because the wife knows everything about the guy—from his ability in bed to the smell of his shit—there's no mystery or excitement and so attraction just dies.

Don't delve into the details. Leave it all to her imagination. This will actually make her *more* likely to want to be the girl(s) you're going out with.

It comes down to this: Preselection (i.e. having other girls attracted to you and dating you) is arguably *the most important key* to escaping the friend zone. It is the secret to making her see you as lover material rather than friend zone material.

You need to be the guy who has options. Having one (or worse, zero!) options when it comes to women gets you shoved in the friend zone faster than you can say "oops!" Meanwhile, she'll go chase that guy who has five different women eagerly pursuing him.

Just as banks only lend money to people that can prove they don't need the bank in the first place, so too do women chase after men that have other options at their disposal. It's just how it works—so use it to your advantage.

So remember, to break out of the friend zone, date other people.

Recreate Yourself

"Law #25: Re-create yourself. Do not accept the roles that society foists on you. Re-create yourself by forging a new identity, one that commands attention and never bores the audience. Be the master of your own image rather than letting others define it for you. Incorporate dramatic devices into your public gestures and actions—your power will be enhanced and your character will seem larger than life."
– Robert Greene, The 48 Laws of Power

A crucial step to getting out of the friend zone is shaking up how your friend sees you.

You must change her perception of you—your place in her mind—in order for there to even be the possibility of her reclassifying you as boyfriend material rather than friend zone material.

Now, I mentioned earlier that a woman's attraction is based more on a man's behavioral traits than his physical traits. This is true. That said, your appearance still plays an important role. If she has a choice of two behaviorally similar men, but one of them has a neckbeard, $5 haircut and oversized clothes while the other wears clothes that fit well and emphasize his physique, has a professional haircut that frames his face nicely, and looks fit with well-defined muscles—then who do you think she's going to choose?

Obviously, she is going to choose the latter guy.

What does this mean for you?

Be Sexy

Hit the gym, get a professional haircut, and wear good-looking clothes that fit you very well. And, if you're overweight, start eating nothing but meat and vegetables. Seriously. A general rule of thumb is that anything that comes in plastic or a box makes you fat.

The key is to shake up her image of you. Her brain has learned to associate your image with whatever preconceived notions she has about you—in your case, that you belong in the friend zone. But by completely shaking up that image, she is forced to recategorize you and what you mean to her.

Develop Dominant Body Language

In addition to better fitting clothes, a flattering new hairstyle, a more impressive physique, and all that good stuff, you need to improve your body language. The fact that you're in the friend zone most likely means that you have nice guy body language. In other words, submissive, weak body language. Think of Marlon Brando's authoritative yet cool body language versus the body language of a first grader being scolded or an awkward wallflower at a party.

I've written an entire book on body language—so there's a lot to it—but the basics are this: You want to have expansive, open body language (as opposed to contractive, closed body language). You want to use your body to take up lots of space. Stand tall, rest your arm on the back of an empty chair next to you, keep your legs apart and make room for your balls, lean back and clasp your hands behind your head and kick your feet up onto the desk/table (if appropriate), etc. Women find expansive, open body language attractive. So don't be afraid to relax, spread your body out, and take up plenty of space.

The problem with most nice guys is their body language is very constrictive. They try to take up as little space as possible. They clench their legs together, keep their elbows at their side, slouch, take little, quick steps, look down at their feet, etc. You do *not* want to display this kind of timid body language. Based on this alone, women will slot you in the friend zone before you've even had a chance to open your mouth.

Define Your Life Mission

Although this seems completely unrelated to escaping the friend zone, having a mission in life will do wonders for your love life.

But what do I mean by mission?

By mission, I mean something you want to achieve with your life. Your contribution to the world. It could be as simple as building a $10,000 a month internet marketing business or it could be as big as ending world hunger or becoming a world tennis champion. Whatever it is, you must have a *burning desire* to achieve it. Your desire must be so great that it is your No. 1 priority in life.

When you have a mission, you don't obsess over women.

When you have a mission, you don't put women on pedestals (the only thing you put on a pedestal is your mission) or act as if you're their servant.

When you have a mission, you gain an inexplicable confidence and charisma. You walk with confidence, your every step has purpose. You start walking, talking, and thinking like a champion. And women love it.

When you have a mission, you have an exciting life of your own. Your life becomes an adventure and women can't help but want to tag along for the ride.

When you have a mission, you start taking charge. You become more of a leader, not just when it comes to your mission, but in all areas of life. You seem to gain an air of authority. People start respecting you more, without even knowing why.

When you have a mission, you're focused, driven, and determined—traits that women find irresistible. You become the master of your fate and the captain of your soul.

Most guys in the friend zone, however, don't have a mission. They don't know their purpose. They just wander around like a lost dog. And when they find an attractive woman, she becomes the center of their life. They start obsessing over her. They hang out with her all the time. They call her for hours and respond to her texts within seconds. They drive her everywhere. They listen to all her problems and put up with all her nonsense. They become lovesick. The vacuum that previously existed (i.e. the absence of a life mission) gets filled by her. She becomes their life. Unfortunately, all of this incredibly unattractive behavior serves only to get him locked in the friend zone.

So get a mission. Find a life purpose.

Negotiating Your Way Out of the Friend Zone (Without Her Knowing)

Before we conclude with the final stage of escaping the friend zone, let's take the chance to examine the art of escaping the friend zone from a different perspective.

You see, there is another way to of looking at the strategies discussed in this book. Rather than just looking at them as ways to get out of the friend zone, you can look at the methods discussed as ways of renegotiating your friendship.

In an article—"Escape the Friend Zone: From Friend to Girlfriend or Boyfriend"—on *Psychology Today*, Jeremy Nicholson looks at the friend zone from a unique perspective. He explains that really, being in the friend zone means that you're in an uneven relationship. One person is getting what they want while the other person is not.

For example, you might be doing everything for your "friend". You buy her things, go places with her, listen to her problems, get her out of trouble, and drive her everywhere. Although you want to be her boyfriend, she isn't interested.

After all, she's already getting all her "boyfriend" needs met by you. She gets everything she wants without giving you what you want. She can get all of your effort while staying free and noncommittal. That's why you're in the friend zone

So how do you escape the friend zone?

First, you must realize that relationships require negotiation. To get what you want—her panties rather than her "guy problems"—you must attempt to re-negotiate. Not by drawing up a contract, but by changing your actions to balance the scales.

How?

Use the strategies discussed in this book.

Be less interested. Desperate, needy people get what others give them, not what they want. You must be willing and able to walk away.

Withdraw attention. Stop buying her stuff, driving her everywhere, instantly answering text messages, and spending 24/7 with her. Your absence will make her miss you and want you more. People value that which is scarce, rare, or has been taken away from them. This will make her more willing to meet your needs back.

Go date other attractive women. In addition to the almost magic powers of preselection discussed earlier, dating other attractive women will create competition. This links into the power of scarcity mentioned in the point above.

Although this perspective presents nothing new, looking at this as a renegotiation of an uneven social exchange might be of help to some of you.

Now, let's move onto the final stage (plus some brief summaries of what has been discussed so far.

Conclusion: Make Your Move

If you do nothing, nothing happens. It's as true when it comes to kicking a ball as it does when guiding a spacecraft to the outer reaches of the solar system.

Consider Newton's third law of motion: "For every action, there is an equal and opposite reaction."

Likewise, when it comes to escaping the friend zone, nothing will happen if you don't do anything. If you just continue doing what you've always been doing, you'll continue to get what you've been getting—the friend zone!

Okay, but what action need you take?

Well first, let's take a quick look at what we've covered so far.

First, you must withdraw your attention. No more being her 24/7 therapist. No more hanging out with her for hours and hours on end. Just disappear for a week. Get busy living your own life. And no, don't *tell* her you're going to be busy/unavailable for a week. Just do it. This will cause her to start thinking about you differently. It will also demonstrate that you're a higher value male—potential lover material, not friend zone material.

Second, when you finally make contact again after your week of total disappearance, **take charge. Lead her.** Come back not as the wussy nice guy that previously commanded your body, but as a leader. A masculine, dominant man who takes charge without so much as a second thought. Don't be bossy— that just comes off as insecure. Just lead. Make decisions. Think in terms of "I'm doing this if you'd care to join" rather than "I'll follow you wherever you go, so please, take charge, I'm too scared to do what I want to do... I'll do whatever you do... what do *you* want to do?" You'll be surprised by how easy it is. Women (and even most men) don't mind tagging along with you—if anything, they probably prefer it to having to make the decisions themselves. Just say what you're going to do and add "if you'd care to join" or "if you want to come." For example, "I'm going to Subway for lunch if you'd care to join" or (if you're in university) "I'm going to the library to do some work if you want to come."

Third, flirt. Remember, keep it subtle. Successful flirting is subtle flirting. Overt flirting is awkward at best and creepy at worst. The two techniques that should help you get started with flirting are:

- Push-pull (i.e. wittily yet subtly imply attraction then playfully tease her—hot and then cold).
- Chase framing (i.e. framing the conversation in a way that implies *she* is the one trying to seduce you and you're just an innocent victim)

Fourth, preselection. Start dating other women. Seems counterintuitive, but it works like magic. Just remember to not tell her any details or specifics about your time with other women. Keep it all a mystery and let her imagination run wild. When she brings is up, just say something to the effect of, "Yeah, I'm seeing some other women," and then change the topic.

Fifth, recreate yourself. Kill your inner nice guy. Start dressing better, get a better haircut, hit the gym, develop powerful body language, and get a life mission, Get busy pursuing your mission and living your own life.

Finally, make your move. But how?

Before we move on, I want to remind you: Making your move does *not* mean giving The Big Confession speech. That will serve only to kill your chances of ever escaping the friend zone.

Instead, you need to boil slowly.

Boil Slowly

Start small and slowly build up, as if boiling a frog. Chuck the frog into boiling water and he jumps out, slowly boil the water and he doesn't notice until it's too late.

So how can you bring the water to a boil and create a

smoking hot sexual relationship?

Completely disappear for a week (get busy with your own life) and come back a masculine man who takes charge and leads (and still disappear every now and then, don't be available 24/7 or with her all the time). Then, start very subtly flirting; be playful. Go start dating a few other women. Post some pictures of you and a few pretty girls on Facebook. Get the magic of preselection working for you. And, remember to keep it as much of a mystery as you can—let her imagination run wild.

Now, this brings us to the final stage—escalating your way out of the friend zone. Flirting is one aspect of this, but there's another: Touch.

<u>Breaking the Touch Barrier</u>

Sexual relationships have a physical side that friendships do not have. What this means is that an important part of wiggling your way out of the friend zone is **breaking the touch barrier**. And no, I don't mean grope her. You must, once again, take the slow boil approach.

Start small. For example, touch her forearm when emphasizing a point (or even better, when you're both laughing or at a high point in the conversation so she associates your touch with positive emotions). Over time, you slowly build it up. You know, hugs, putting your arm around her, hand on back to guide her, taking lint off her shit, smelling her, adjusting her hair, and so on.

That said, it is important you escalate congruently. By that I mean, you need to start being more playful and flirtatious as well. If you start escalating physically but continue to act as you've always been acting—friend zone material—well, that's just... weird... and kind of awkward. Also, you can—and should —touch her a lot when flirting. Give her a playful shove, high five, palm reading, playing five little piggies, hand on shoulder when laughing, and so on.

Just as important is being aware of whether or not she is comfortable. Pay attention to how she reacts when you touch her, how much she lets you touch her, and whether or not she reciprocates. If she tenses or moves when you touch her or just seems uncomfortable, stop, take it down a notch, and see if you can gradually work your way back up.

If she's comfortable with it (or even better, appears to enjoy it and is reciprocating), then great! Continue to gradually work your way up. Hugging her, tickling her (works well when playfully teasing/flirting with her), putting your hand on her thigh (when sitting), massaging her, and even *gasp* holding her hand. Once again, be aware of how she responds. If she seems uncomfortable, tenses, or makes an effort to move, take it down a notch and see if you can gradually work your way back up.

Obviously, if all this goes well and she's comfortable at this level (putting you arm around her, putting your hand on her thigh, holding her hand, etc.), continue to gradually build the sexual tension.

Sealing the Deal

The next step: Progress to the kiss. If she has been reacting positively and reciprocating so far, you should be good to go. That said, don't go for it in a public place as she will likely shy away. Instead, you'll have a better chance in a private place.

For example, if she's walking around your/her apartment (e.g. getting drinks or food, looking at something, etc.), slowly approach from behind, touch her hips, move close to her ear, smell her, and then brush her hair to the side and kiss or bite her neck.

And, as always, if she responds positively to this (which you will be able to tell by her body language—don't *ask* her for crying out loud!) then continue to progress—either to a full on makeout session and/or sex.

Printed in Great Britain
by Amazon